NOTE TO PARENTS

This book is part of PICTUREPEDIA, a completely
new kind of information series for children.
Its unique combination of pictures and words
encourages children to use their eyes to discover and
explore the world, while introducing them to a wealth
of basic knowledge. Clear, straightforward text
explains each picture thoroughly and provides
additional information about the topic.

"Looking it up" becomes an easy task with
PICTUREPEDIA, an ideal first reference for all types of
schoolwork. Because PICTUREPEDIA is also entertaining,
children will enjoy reading its words and looking
at its pictures over and over again. You can encourage
and stimulate further inquiry by helping your child
pose simple questions for the whole family to
"look up" and answer together.

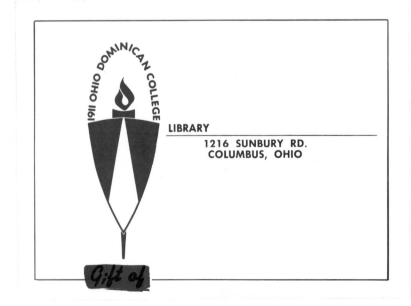

ARTS AND ENTERTAINMENT

DK

A DORLING KINDERSLEY BOOK
Conceived, edited, and designed by DK Direct Limited

Writer Adrian Gilbert
Project Editor Sarah Miller
Art Editor Andrew Walker
U.S. Editor B. Alison Weir
Series Editor Sarah Phillips
Series Art Editor Paul Wilkinson
Picture Researcher Miriam Sharland
Production Manager Ian Paton
Production Assistant Harriet Maxwell
Editorial Director Jonathan Reed
Design Director Ed Day

First American edition, 1993
4 6 8 10 9 7 5 3
Published in the United States by
Dorling Kindersley, Inc., 232 Madison Avenue
New York, New York 10016

Library of Congress Cataloging-in-Publication Data
Arts and Entertainment. — 1st Amer. ed.
p. cm. — (Picturepedia)
Includes index.
ISBN 1-56458-388-0
1. Arts—Juvenile literature. [1. Arts.] I. Series.
NX833.A78 1993
700—dc20   93-2390
                                                                      CIP
                                                                      AC

Reproduced by Colourscan, Singapore
Printed and bound in Italy by Graphicom

ARTS AND ENTERTAINMENT

DK

DORLING KINDERSLEY

LONDON • NEW YORK
STUTTGART

CONTENTS

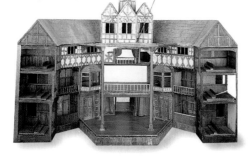

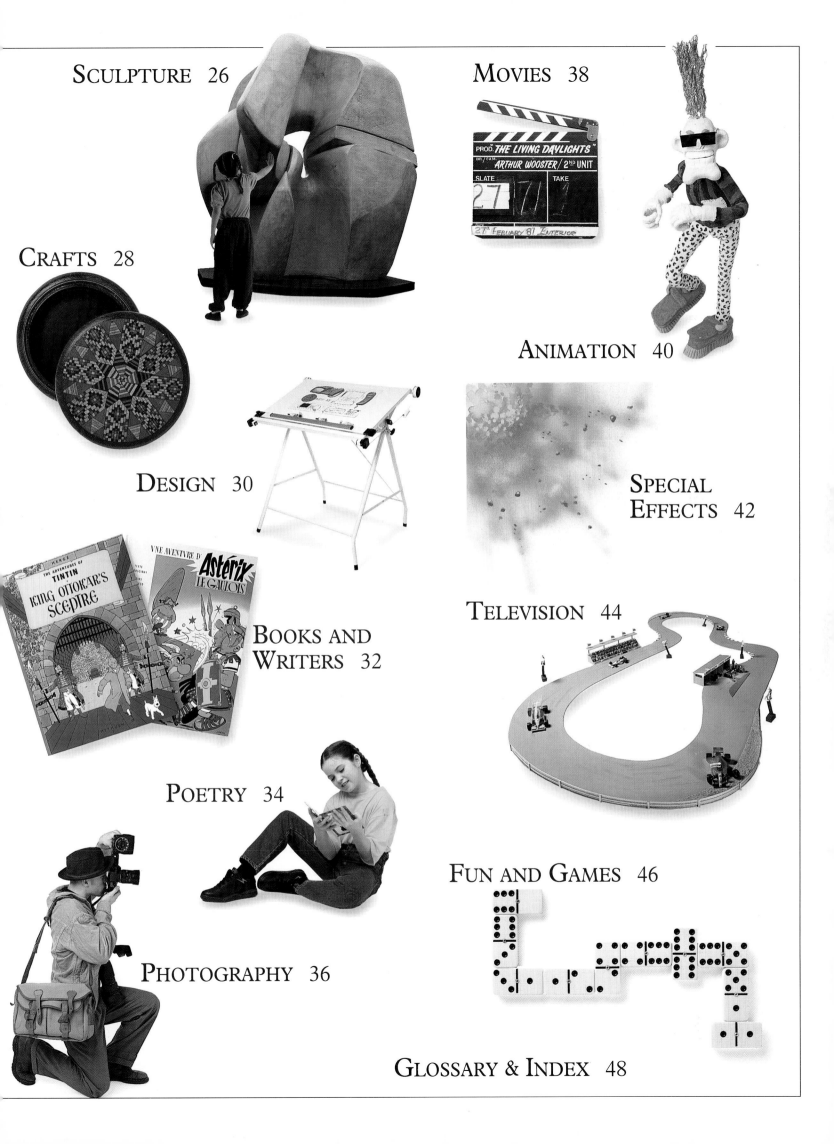

THE CIRCUS

There were circuses in ancient Rome: gladiators fought, chariots raced, and exotic beasts prowled around a sandy, circular arena. But when the Roman empire collapsed, the entertainment ended. The circus did not open again until 1769, when Philip Astley, a bareback horse rider, set up a show in London, England. Gladiators and chariots were replaced by amazing acrobats, fabulous fire-eaters, and silly clowns.

Platform

Clowning Around
There are two different kinds of clowns. White-faced clowns are clever, wear pointed hats, and are called "Joey." They work with red-nosed, foolish clowns, called "Auguste" clowns. All clowns put on their own makeup. No two look exactly alike.

Auguste clowns wear bright, baggy clothes.

Many clowns play musical instruments.

Jugglers use clubs, balls, rings, and even knives!

This one-wheeled bike is called a unicycle. It is difficult to ride.

Clowns first entered the circus ring in 1769.

The best jugglers can keep six or seven clubs in the air at a time.

People laugh when clowns trip over their huge shoes.

In the Middle Ages, jugglers entertained in royal courts.

Some fliers can spin around four times before they are caught.

Legs hold on tightly.

The catcher wraps bandages around his wrists for the flier to grip onto.

Hold On Tight
Trapeze artists swing through the air about 30 ft (10 m) above the ground. If they fall, they are caught in a big net.

Step Right Up!
Brightly colored posters are put up to tell everyone about the show.

The Big Top
Some circuses stay in one place, but most travel from town to town. They are held inside an arena or a tent, called a big top.

Fire-eaters put out the flames by closing their mouths! The flames go out because they need oxygen to burn.

Everyone who hears the drum and sees the parade knows that the circus is in town.

Knife-throwers throw sharp knives at people! They practice a lot to make sure that they always just miss.

Acrobats entertained the crowds in ancient Rome, too.

Acrobats can walk on their hands!

The ringmaster is in charge of the circus.

PUPPETS

Puppets are not a new invention. They were used in ancient Egypt over 2,500 years ago to tell stories. For hundreds of years, Indian puppets have acted out very long tales about the incredible lives of kings and queens. In Europe, during the Middle Ages, puppets helped people understand Bible stories. Today, puppets still entertain people. It can be hard to make a string puppet, or marionette, move properly. Glove, rod, and shadow puppets are much simpler.

Punch

Ten strings move this marionette. Imagine how difficult it is to make it walk and wave at the same time.

If you pull this string, you make the arm move up.

You put your hand inside a glove puppet to make it move.

Hand in Glove
Punch and Judy are famous glove puppets. Their story was first told in Italy over 200 years ago. They are still popular in Britain.

Mrs. Judy Punch

The crocodile bites Punch!

Every marionette has a different face – some are happy, others are sad.

Many marionettes are carved from lime wood.

Crocodile   Policeman

8

This bar moves the legs.

Wire extensions move the hands.

The marionettes are brought to life by moving a device, called a control.

A bar moves the head from side to side.

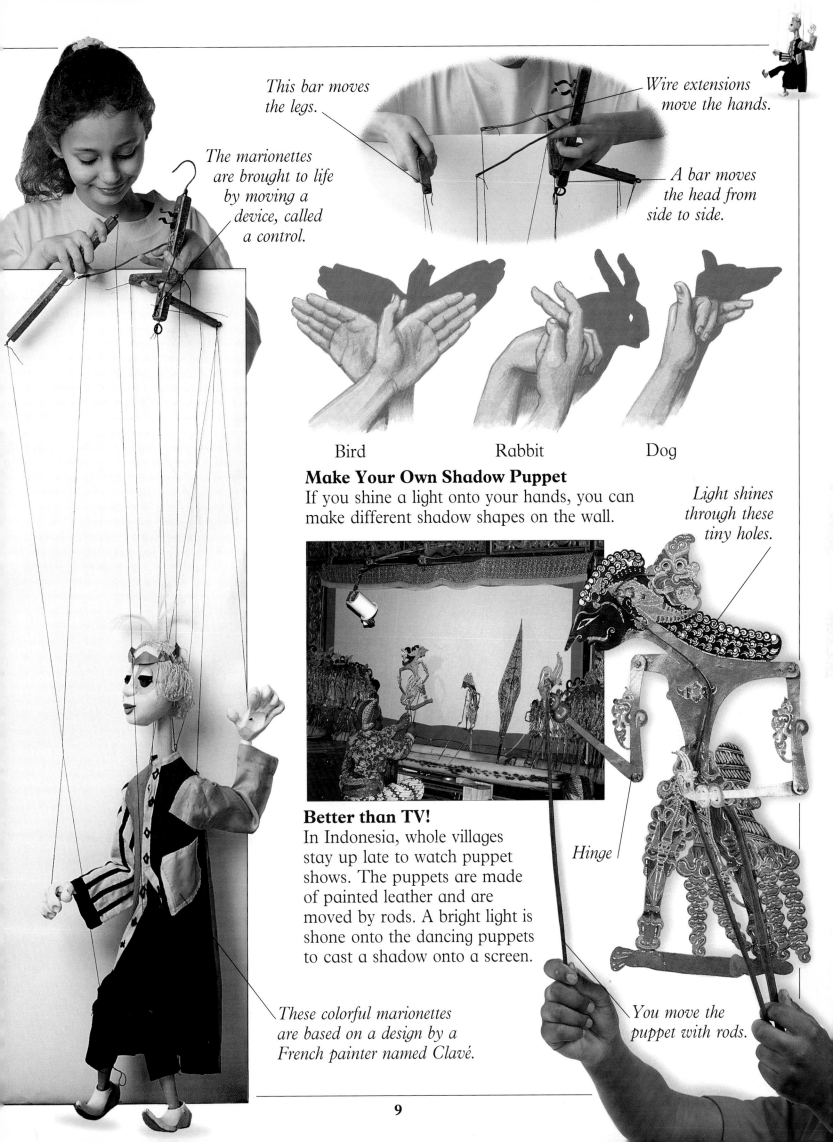

Bird   Rabbit   Dog

Make Your Own Shadow Puppet

If you shine a light onto your hands, you can make different shadow shapes on the wall.

Light shines through these tiny holes.

Better than TV!

In Indonesia, whole villages stay up late to watch puppet shows. The puppets are made of painted leather and are moved by rods. A bright light is shone onto the dancing puppets to cast a shadow onto a screen.

Hinge

These colorful marionettes are based on a design by a French painter named Clavé.

You move the puppet with rods.

THEATERS

People have enjoyed going to the theater to watch plays for centuries. The first theaters were built by the Greeks about 2,500 years ago. Stone seats were carved into a hillside. The actors did not need microphones, because sound carried right up to the back row. Until the 17th century, most plays were staged in the open air. But by the 1650s, bare stages had been replaced by elaborate sets that had to be kept inside, so indoor theaters became common. Lights transformed theaters, too. Realistic acting began with the invention of limelight – for the first time, players' expressions could be seen.

Wagons Roll
In the Middle Ages, actors took their shows, called miracle plays, from town to town. These plays were about the battle between good and evil.

The upper gallery was about 26 feet (8 meters) above the ground.

Stage door

The Globe Theater was built in 1599.

Ancient Art
Noh is an old, traditional type of Japanese theater. Religious stories and ancient myths are performed on a stage that has very little scenery. The plays, some of which are more than 500 years old, can go on for as long as six hours!

More than 2,000 people could crowd in to watch a good play. Only a few could afford to sit in these galleries.

The Globe Theater

William Shakespeare, the most famous of all playwrights, acted on the Globe's wooden stage.

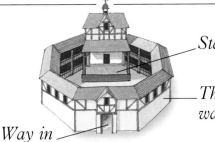

Stage

Way in

The Globe was circular.

Musicians played on this balcony.

When the flag was raised, people knew that a play was going to be performed.

There was no scenery on the stage.

This model of the Globe Theater has been cut in half to let you see inside.

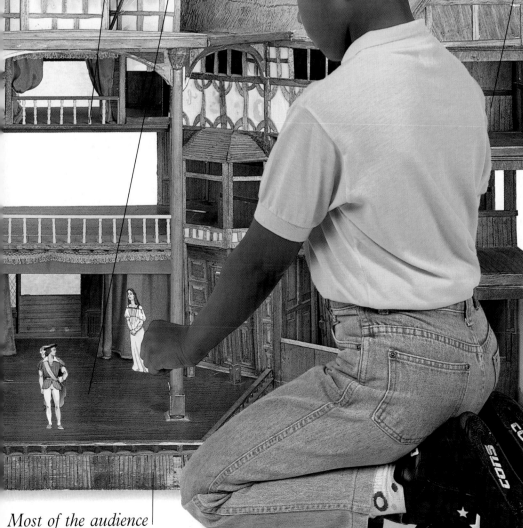

Most of the audience stood around the stage. These "groundlings" got wet when it rained.

Setting the Scene

Theaters come in all sorts of shapes and sizes. Early ones were open to the air. Most modern stages have roofs so that plays can be staged when it is raining.

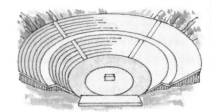

Greek theater
200 BC

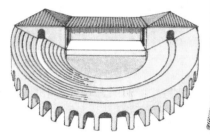

Roman theater
AD 100

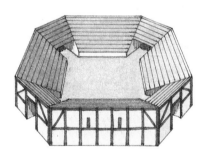

Elizabethan theater
16th century

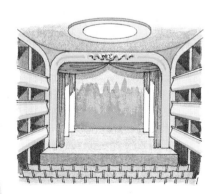

"Modern" theater
19th century

PLAYS AND PLAYERS

Not a Word
Marcel Marceau is a famous French mime artist – he acts out stories without speaking.

Playwrights write stories, or plays, that are performed on stage by players, called actors and actresses. Molière and Shakespeare both lived more than 300 years ago, but their plays, such as *L'Avare* and *Macbeth,* are still popular. Laurence Olivier, one of this century's most famous actors, starred in *Henry V* by Shakespeare and also in more modern plays, such as *The Entertainer* by John Osborne. Like all good players, he could make an audience believe that what they are seeing is real, not just an act.

The actor playing Romeo shows that he likes Juliet by giving her a rose.

The players wear costumes like those worn by rich Italians in the past.

Happy Ending
Plays that make people laugh are called comedies. Molière wrote many wonderful plays in the 17th century that are still funny today.

Sad Ending
Tragedies are plays with sad endings. *Cat on a Hot Tin Roof* was written by Tennessee Williams and is a famous modern tragedy.

Setting the Scene

Romeo and Juliet is one of Shakespeare's saddest plays. The couple can never be together because their families hate one another.

These are the first words Romeo ever says to Juliet.

Juliet replies. She is not upset with him for holding her hand.

ROMEO (*to Juliet, touching her hand*)
If I profane with my unworthiest hand
This holy shrine, the gentle sin is this:
My lips, two blushing pilgrims, ready stand
To smooth that rough touch with a tender kiss.   95

JULIET
Good pilgrim, you do wrong your hand too much,
Which mannerly devotion shows in this;
For saints have hands that pilgrims' hands do touch,

This line is not spoken – it tells the actors what to do.

There are 145 lines in this scene, or part of the play. This is line 95.

The actress pretends to be shy, yet pleased to receive the rose.

Makeup Magic

To make an audience believe what they are seeing, players often change the way they look by using makeup.

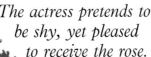

Young

Talcum powder and special white mascara makes brown hair and eyebrows look gray.

Going gray

Pale powder takes away the rosy cheeks.

Lines are drawn on the face with a special dark pencil.

Old

Staged in the East

Spectacular, traditional Chinese plays are known as Peking opera in the West. Every action and color has a special meaning. Blue and yellow costumes show that a person is bad tempered and proud.

MUSIC

Musical sounds can be made with your voice or by playing an instrument. The first instruments were played more than 35,000 years ago – people blew into shells and hollow mammoth bones! Today's instruments are more complicated. The sounds they make can be high or low. This is known as the pitch of the note. The way these sounds are arranged is called the tune. Rhythm is the pattern of long and short notes. A skillful musician can make the same tune sound slow and sleepy or loud and jazzy!

Beat the Clock?
A metronome can tick at different speeds. Musicians listen to it to make sure they are playing at the right speed. This is called keeping the beat.

Stylish Groups

Jazz band

Pop group

String quartet

Wired for Sound
Electronic instruments are actually almost silent! When you twang the steel strings on an electric guitar, they vibrate. This movement is changed into tiny electrical signals by pickups beneath the strings. These signals are then increased by an amplifier and finally turned into sounds by a loudspeaker.

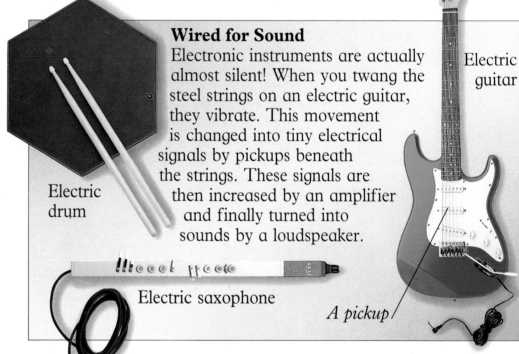

Electric guitar

Electric drum

Electric saxophone

A pickup

Note It Down
Music is written down in a special language. Instead of words, there are notes. The notes are named after letters of the alphabet.

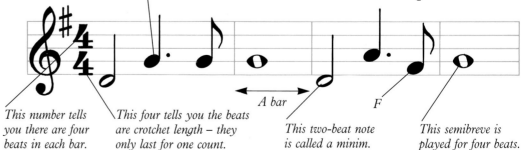

Higher notes are written on higher lines.

A bar

F

This number tells you there are four beats in each bar.

This four tells you the beats are crotchet length – they only last for one count.

This two-beat note is called a minim.

This semibreve is played for four beats.

Bagpipes

You blow here.

A World of Music
Different countries and regions have very different instruments and styles of music. This traditional music is played by local people, or folk, so it is often called folk music.

Banjo

Scotland is famous for bagpipes. They are played by blowing air into a bag and then squeezing the air up through the pipes.

People who live in the eastern mountains of the United States are famous for their banjo playing. Banjos were first brought to the United States by enslaved Africans.

Panpipes are made from pipes of different lengths and are popular in South America. You play them by blowing over the top of the pipes. Longer pipes make lower sounds.

Panpipes

Australian aboriginals are the only people who play the didgeridoo. It is usually made from a hollow bamboo branch and is difficult to play.

Didgeridoo

ORCHESTRAS

Many musicians play music in groups, called orchestras. Most orchestras have four sections: string, percussion, woodwind, and brass. The different sounds and notes, from as many as 120 instruments in a symphony orchestra, combine to form marvelous music. Orchestras usually play classical music, often written by great composers of the past, such as Mozart and Beethoven.

Percussion players play many different instruments, such as drums, triangles, and gongs.

Cymbal

Principal violinist

Clarinet

Violin

Sounds Different
Most of the instruments in a gamelan orchestra are percussion instruments – there are no violins or cellos at all. This music comes from Indonesia.

The leader of an orchestra is always a violin player who sits near the conductor.

Woodwind instruments, including recorders, are played by blowing down a tube that has holes in it.

The conductor stands in front of the musicians so that they can see the baton.

The French horn, like the trumpet and trombone, is a long, curving tube that is made of brass.

Bow

Two beats to a bar

Three beats to a bar

Four beats to a bar

Keeping the Beat

If all the instruments in an orchestra played at different speeds, they would sound dreadful. The musicians keep in time by watching a conductor, who waves a baton to the beat of the music.

Conductor

Short stick, called a baton

This cello, like the violin, is part of the string section. It is played by drawing a bow across the strings.

Which Section?

The clarinet player is sitting on a yellow seat. By using the key shown below, you can see that a clarinet is a woodwind instrument.

Strings

☐ String ☐ Percussion ☐ Woodwind ☐ Brass

Child Genius

Wolfgang Amadeus Mozart wrote, or composed, over 600 pieces of music. He completed his first symphony when he was eight years old!

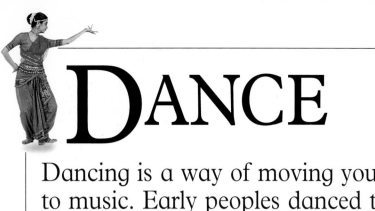

DANCE

Dancing is a way of moving your body in time to music. Early peoples danced to please their gods. Today, most people dance purely for fun. It was not until the 12th century that dancing in pairs became popular. The arrival of the waltz in the 1800s was shocking – it was the first time that couples had held one another closely as they danced. A revolution has taken place this century, too – set steps have been replaced by solo dancers who make up all their own moves.

This is an imaginary "bow."

The dancer pulls back an "arrow."

There are more than 25 different finger positions. Each one has a different meaning.

Proud to Dance
The spectacular flamenco dance comes from the gypsy peoples of Spain. The dancers hold their heads up high as they stamp their feet and turn around. The women wear long, colorful dresses, but the men wear black.

Head over Heels
Jive dancing has few rules. The dancers twist, spin, jump, leap around – whatever the music makes them feel like doing!

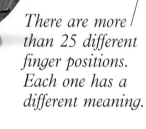

Taking a bow

The dance begins

Taps are fitted to the heel and toe of each shoe.

Tap, Tap, Tap
Fred Astaire was one of the most famous dancers of this century. He tap-danced his way through many shows and movies. Small pieces of metal, called taps, were fixed to the soles of his shoes. When his feet touched the ground, you could hear the quick clatter of clicking metal.

A classical Indian dancer uses the whole of the body. The neck, wrists, and even the eyes move to the rhythm of the music.

As she pretends to put a clip in her hair, the dancer looks into the "mirror."

Her hand is held out flat to form a "mirror!"

Moves Matter
Classical Indian dance has been performed for more than 1,000 years. Sometimes the dancers just create shapes and patterns with their bodies. In other dances, they use hand movements and mime to tell stories of Hindu gods.

She stamps her bare foot in time to the drumbeat of an instrument, called a tabla.

The pleats in the special dance dress let the dancer move freely.

One, Two, Three
The waltz is danced in triple time – each bar of music has three beats. As the dancers swirl around and around, they draw their feet together once every three steps.

BALLET

At the Bar
Ballet dancers must warm up their muscles before they dance. They do this by stretching while holding onto a pole, called a bar.

Ballet is a graceful type of dance that mimes stories to music. It began in Italy, but was developed into the style you see today by the French. King Louis XIV of France started the first ballet school in 1661. But the dancers in these "ballets" at the French court sang and recited poems! The first true ballet, without words, was not performed until 1789. The basic steps and jumps taught by King Louis's school are still used today, which is why many of them have French names. *Glisser* means to glide and *pas de chat* means "step of the cat"!

Louis XIV

This short, stiff skirt is called a tutu. It allows the dancer's legs to be seen.

Hopping Frogs
The Tales of Beatrix Potter is an amazing ballet. The dancers wear wonderful costumes and animal masks.

Women did not dance in ballets until 1681. Then, they had to wear long, flowing dresses.

"Turning feet out" takes years of practice.

First position
(*en première*)

Second position
(*en seconde*)

Third position
(*en troisième*)

Fourth position
(*en quatrième*)

Fifth position
(*en cinquième*)

The Five Positions
In the 17th century, a ballet teacher called Beauchamps developed five foot and arm positions that enabled dancers to keep their balance and still look elegant. Most ballet steps begin or end with one of these positions.

Long hair is always tied back in a bun.

Male dancers need to be strong. They have to lift ballerinas high up in the air.

This Is Ballet, Too!

During this century, some very adventurous ballets have been performed. These modern ballets use many of the classic steps, but often have no story. The imaginatively dressed dancers simply express a mood.

Ballerinas sew on their own ribbons.

The ballerina keeps her foot pointed.

The leg is held very still and straight.

A female ballet dancer is called a ballerina.

Dancing on tiptoes makes the ballerina's legs look longer and more graceful.

Ballerinas put cotton inside their shoes to keep their toes from hurting.

Ballet dancers wear tights.

Ballet Shoes

To dance on tiptoe, or *en pointe*, ballerinas wear special satin slippers with stiffened toes. Girls have to be at least twelve years old before their feet are strong enough to dance like this.

Male dancers' shoes do not have stiffened toes.

OPERA

Inside Paris opera house

Operas mix music with theater in a very spectacular way. The performers on stage act out a story, but instead of speaking the words, they sing them. A performance usually begins with an overture. This is a piece of catchy music that features snatches of the tunes that will be heard during the rest of the opera. As well as singing the story, the stars on the stage also perform solo songs, called arias. These are often the most beautiful songs.

Smashing Note
When you rub your finger around the rim of a glass, it makes a high sound. If a person with a strong voice sings this high note loudly, and for a long time, the sound waves can shatter the glass!

Stylish Surroundings
Operas are usually staged in special buildings that are designed to help the whole audience hear the sound clearly. The Sydney Opera House in Australia is one of the most modern. It was finished in 1973.

Paris opera house

The jagged roof looks like waves or the sails on a yacht.

Just one of the two main halls holds 1,500 people.

Sydney Opera House

Crowded Stage

Operas sometimes have spectacular stage sets and, as well as the soloists, a large group of singers, called the chorus.

Dressed to Impress

Opera singers wear incredible costumes to play their parts. In *The Cunning Little Vixen*, their makeup is amazing, too.

A Choice of Voices

The soprano is the highest female voice. It is a brilliant and exciting sound.

The contralto, or alto, has a slightly lower voice than the soprano. It has a warmer tone.

Tenors sing many of the important male songs in an opera.

The bass sings the lowest notes, and his voice is deep and strong.

On Song

Luciano Pavarotti's voice is powerful and beautiful. He is one of the world's greatest tenors.

Operas are mostly sung in Italian, French, or German.

Powerful lungs enable the singers to sing without a microphone!

Foxy Tale

Operas tell stories. *The Cunning Little Vixen* by Leoš Janaćěk is about a crafty female fox who escapes from a forester and has many exciting adventures.

PAINTING

This says "Jan van Eyck was here, 1434." It may be to prove the artist was a witness to the marriage.

This cave painting is believed to be 30,000 years old.

Many thousands of years ago, people painted pictures of bulls, horses, and antelopes on the walls of their caves. We will never be sure why they did this – perhaps it was to make magic and bring people luck in their hunting. Since then, artists have painted pictures to record events, to honor heroes and heroines, to make people wonder about the world, to tell stories, or simply for pleasure. All artists have their own painting styles, and you may not like them all – it's up to you.

If you look closely in the mirror, you can see the reflections of two other people. Perhaps one is the artist himself.

Hills and Valleys
Paintings of the countryside are called landscapes. This Chinese scene looks very different from a Western landscape. It is painted on silk, using a fine and detailed style.

Things that are farther away look smaller, so the artist has made the shoes at the front bigger than those at the back. This gives the picture depth.

King Ramses II

by an unknown Egyptian artist

Lucrezia Panciatichi

by Il Bronzino

Self-portrait

by Vincent van Gogh

Woman Weeping

by Pablo Picasso

The Arnolfini Marriage, painted by Jan van Eyck in 1434

Looking for Clues

This painting records a couple's marriage. But if you look closely, you will see it is much more than just a wedding picture.

One candle is left to burn, even though it is daylight, to show that the couple will always love one another.

Like the merchant, his wife is wearing expensive clothes. It was the fashion to hold skirts in this way.

Action Painting

In this painting, the modern American artist, Jackson Pollock, was not trying to show objects or people, but feelings. He worked by dripping and splattering paint on the canvas.

Son of Man

by René Magritte

Marilyn Monroe

by Andy Warhol

The light shines on the couple's hands, and the artist has shown every tiny line.

Painting Portraits

For thousands of years, artists have enjoyed painting pictures of people. Not all of them painted the person true to life – there are many different styles of painting.

SCULPTURE

Sculptures are three-dimensional, not flat like paintings. Bricks, plastic, even rubber tires have all been used by sculptors, but the traditional materials are wood, stone, and clay. Some sculptors build up their image by adding small pieces of material, such as clay. Others start with a big block of wood or stone and cut away, or subtract, material. When Michelangelo carved, he believed he was setting free a stone person, or statue, that was trapped inside the stone!

Mystery from the Past
Strange statues were carved on Easter Island more than 1,000 years ago. Nobody knows for sure what they were for, or how they were built.

Many of Moore's sculptures are based on natural shapes, such as smooth pebbles.

In Touch with Nature
The sculptures of Henry Moore (1898-1986) don't always look like everyday things. Some just make the space they occupy look more interesting.

This rounded sculpture is meant to be touched.

If you walk around this sculpture, you see different, exciting shapes.

Mountain Men
Mount Rushmore has the heads of four American presidents cut into it. It took 14 years to blast and drill presidents Washington, Jefferson, Roosevelt, and Lincoln out of the rock.

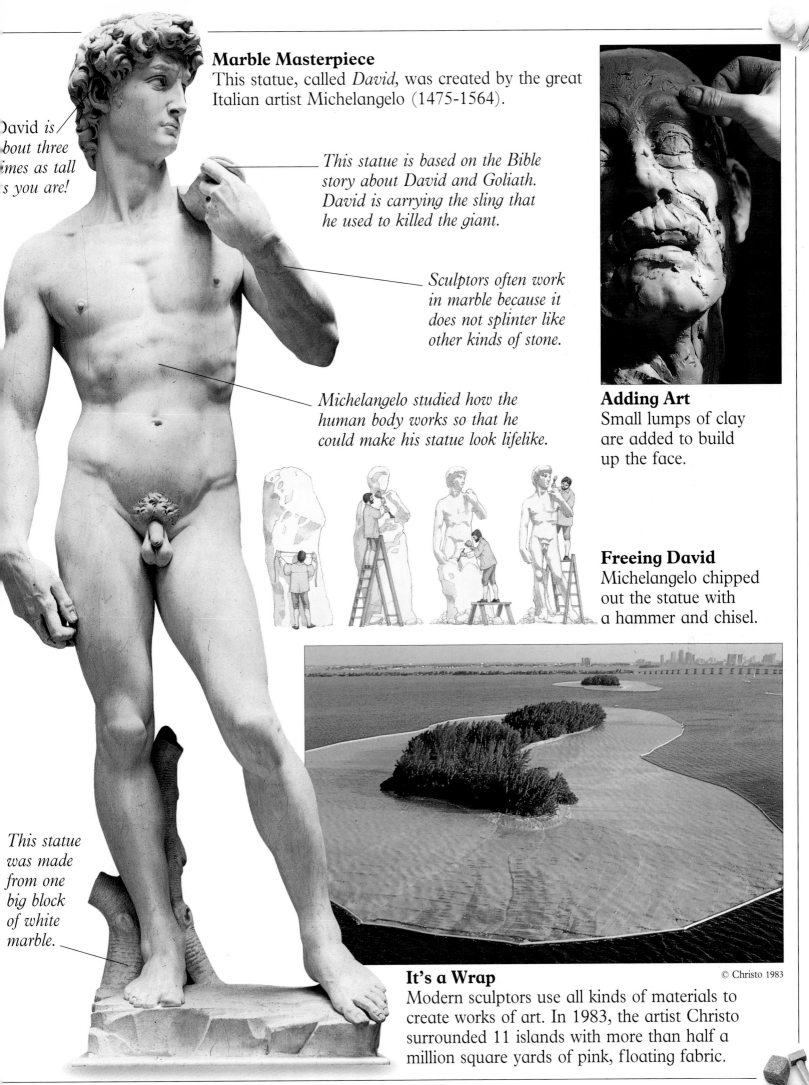

Marble Masterpiece
This statue, called *David*, was created by the great Italian artist Michelangelo (1475-1564).

David is about three times as tall as you are!

This statue is based on the Bible story about David and Goliath. David is carrying the sling that he used to killed the giant.

Sculptors often work in marble because it does not splinter like other kinds of stone.

Michelangelo studied how the human body works so that he could make his statue look lifelike.

Adding Art
Small lumps of clay are added to build up the face.

Freeing David
Michelangelo chipped out the statue with a hammer and chisel.

This statue was made from one big block of white marble.

It's a Wrap
© Christo 1983
Modern sculptors use all kinds of materials to create works of art. In 1983, the artist Christo surrounded 11 islands with more than half a million square yards of pink, floating fabric.

CRAFTS

Most things you use or wear are made by machines. But until about 200 years ago, almost everything was made, or crafted, by hand – from simple pots to complicated patterns of lace. No two handmade objects are the same. Every Persian carpet, for example, is knotted into a slightly different pattern. This difference, and the skill it takes to create a well-crafted object, is what keeps crafts popular in a "machine-made" world.

A Good Egg!
Peter Carl Fabergé made fabulous eggs decorated with gold and jewels. They were given by Russian royalty as Easter presents.

Wiry Work
The ancient Greeks and Romans both used filigree to make delicate jewelry. Today, craftsmen still make wonderful shapes by curling, twisting, and plaiting thin wires of silver or gold.

The wires are joined together by being melted.

This pot will be coated with glaze – a liquid that will make it smooth, shiny, and waterproof.

Silver is a bright metal and is often used to make jewelry.

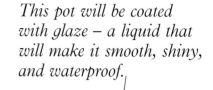

Silver wire

Throwing a Pot
To make a pot, you first throw a lump of clay onto a turning wheel and then mold it into shape. The clay is then hardened by baking, or firing, in a hot oven, called a kiln.

Threads of silver wrap around the turquoise stone.

Pearl

The pot is painted after it has been baked.

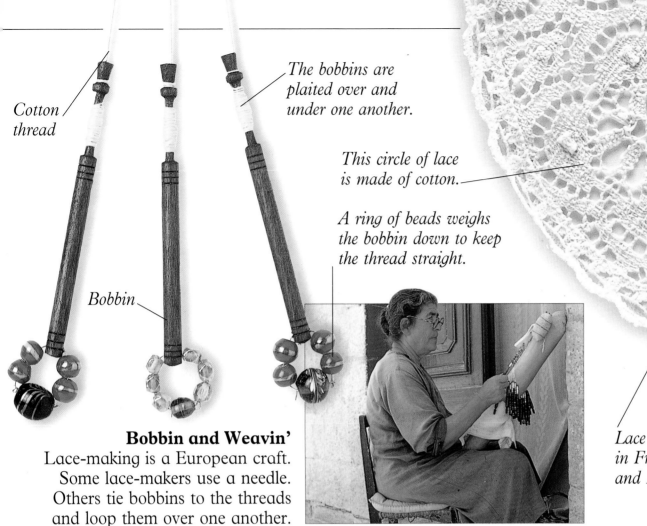

Cotton thread

The bobbins are plaited over and under one another.

This circle of lace is made of cotton.

Bobbin

A ring of beads weighs the bobbin down to keep the thread straight.

Bobbin and Weavin'
Lace-making is a European craft. Some lace-makers use a needle. Others tie bobbins to the threads and loop them over one another.

Lace is made mostly in France, Belgium, and Britain.

This dark wood is called ebony.

The slices of wood are tiny – the whole box is less than four inches (ten centimeters) wide.

Thin pieces of oak are dyed different colors.

Making a Mark
Marquetry is a way of decorating wooden objects by making a jigsaw puzzle of different colored woods. Thin slices of wood are glued together to make up the pattern.

Magic Carpets
It takes many months for skilled weavers to weave and knot dyed wool or soft silk into a magnificent, colorful carpet. The best carpets are made in Persia, now called Iran, and China.

This Persian carpet is made of sheep's wool.

DESIGN

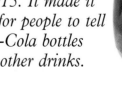

Metal and modern plastic lids are designed to keep in the fizz and to be easy to open.

You may not realize it, but most of the things around you have been carefully designed. Kettles are shaped so that they do not drip boiling water, telephones are easy to hold – even pegs and pens are designed! The job of the designer is to decide on the best shape, size, color, and material to make an object that looks good and works well. A good design can last for many years, but many everyday objects change to match people's changing taste. People used to like to wear top hats – now they prefer caps!

The shapes of letters can be designed – the fancy writing of the word "Coca-Cola" is known all over the world. It was designed in 1886.

This word needs to be easy to read, so the shape is simple. It would have been harder to read like this: bottle

The ridges and the curves on this bottle make it easy to hold.

The first Coca-Cola bottles had straight sides. This curved bottle was designed in 1915. It made it easy for people to tell Coca-Cola bottles from other drinks.

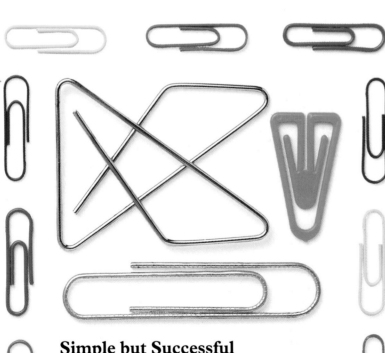

Simple but Successful

Paper clips are cleverly designed to hold sheets of paper together. They come in many shapes and sizes, but the original style is still used the most because it is well designed.

Thick glass is strong. A Coke bottle can be refilled and reused.

Taking Shape

This designer is using Computer Aided Design, called CAD. He is creating a car shape that can slip through the air at high speed. It's quicker, and cheaper, to do this on a computer than to build and test a lot of real cars.

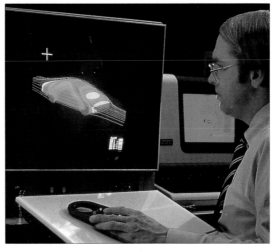

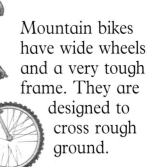

The Moulton bike was designed in the 1960s. It had very small wheels and a low frame so that it could fold up!

Mountain bikes have wide wheels and a very tough frame. They are designed to cross rough ground.

Ring-pulls used to be dropped on the ground as litter. Designers solved this messy problem by developing an opener that stays on the can.

A clever little "lip" stops your drink from dripping.

Racing bikes are designed to win races! Steel is heavy, so they are made of light carbon fiber.

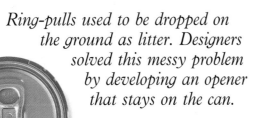

Millions to Make

By 1960, demand for a nonreturnable container was so great that Coca-Cola brought out a can. Today, 500 million people drink Coke every day!

Air can rush past this shaped helmet.

The famous, flowing script is still used.

Designers use color. Coke cans are red because this bright color has been linked with Coca-Cola for years.

The can is shaped from one piece of metal, so it is cheap to make.

The can is light, easy to carry, and can be recycled.

What to Wear?

Fashion designers create clothes. They decide what people will want to be seen wearing, the shape of the outfit, and which material will work best.

BOOKS AND WRITERS

Even though we live in the age of television and radio, books are still a very important way of telling people about the world. There are two different types of books: fiction books are stories that have been made up by an author; nonfiction books are about real things and people. This is a nonfiction book. When the words have been written, they are often placed on the page with photos and illustrations. Pictures, as well as words, provide information.

Photos

Illustrators and photographers are organized by the designer.

Instructions for the printer

A designer plans how the book will look.

Pencil Drawings
The editor, author, and designer decide what should go on the page. The designer then draws a "rough" of what the words and pictures will look like.

Teamwork
Many people work together to produce a book.

Taking Shape
Photographs and illustrations are positioned on the page and sent to be printed.

Waiting for Words
The printers produce a page without words.

Picture researcher

Author

Illustrator

Photographer

Using Your Imagination

Imagination is a writer's most important tool. Words can describe incredible things. In his book *Twenty Thousand Leagues under the Sea*, Jules Verne created amazing adventures – brave divers battled with giant sharks and squid!

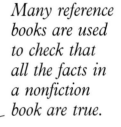

Famous Fiction Writers

Hans Christian Andersen
(1805-1875)

Mark Twain
(1835-1910)

Roald Dahl
(1916-1990)

Photos are looked at on a light box to check that they are in focus.

The text is typed into a computer. This makes it simple to change sentences and move paragraphs around.

The editor looks after all the words in the book. They have to be easy to read and spelled correctly.

Many reference books are used to check that all the facts in a nonfiction book are true.

Dictionary

All these objects have been photographed for this book. They are called props.

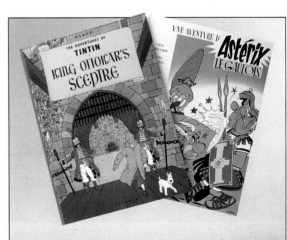

Picture Books
Comics, such as *Astérix* and *Tintin*, tell stories through pictures. The words are often written inside speech bubbles.

POETRY

Scene from the *Iliad*

A poem is a pleasing pattern of words. The words are picked for how they sound, not just what they mean. Some poems, such as "Jabberwocky" by Lewis Carroll, are full of nonsense! One of the earliest poems, the *Iliad* by Homer, is incredibly long, but the rhythm of its words makes it easier to remember. Poetry began when there was no writing – stories could not be read, so they had to be learned by heart. Today, poems are written because they are enjoyable to read and hear.

Historic Hiawatha?
The famous poem Hiawatha, by the American poet Henry Wadsworth Longfellow, is mostly a made-up story. There was a real Hiawatha, though, who led the Native American Iroquois tribe during the 1500s.

Poetry to Music
Magical poems by T.S. Eliot, such as "Macavity: The Mystery Cat" and "The Song of the Jellicles," have been made into the musical *Cats*.

I'm
part of a
project on flight.
I'm supposed to attain
a great height. But
unfortunately
I got stuck
in a tree
so
it
looks
like
I'm
here
for
the
night!

Short and Sweet
Haikus are Japanese poems with only three lines – you should be able to say the poem in one breath. This haiku was written by Basho, the most famous haiku poet.

咲きみだす桃の中より初櫻

From among the peach trees
Blooming everywhere,
The first cherry blossoms.

Light Verse
The shape of a poem can be as important as the words. In this poem, long lines form the shape of a kite, and small words at the end make the tail.

What's in a Poem?
Poets use a number of ways to arrange their words.

Many poems are divided into groups of lines, called verses.

The poet could have said that a bicycle bell has a sharp sound, but it is more interesting to say that it is as clear as an icicle.

"Bells"

Hard as crystal,
   Clear as an icicle,
Is the tinkling sound
   Of a bell on a bicycle.

All in the Mind
Poets use words to paint pictures in the mind. William Wordsworth began one poem with "I wandered lonely as a cloud." He could have said "I was on my own," but this is not so descriptive.

Words at the ends of lines, such as "shelf" and "itself," sound the same. This is called rhyming.

The bell in the clock
   That stands on the shelf,
Slowly, sleepily
   Talks to itself.

The school bell is noisy
   And bangs like brass.
"Hurry up! Hurry up!
   Late for class!"

Faster than fairies,
   faster than witches,
Bridges and houses,
   hedges and ditches;
And charging along like
   troops in a battle,
All through the meadows
   the horses and cattle

Poets choose the words in their poems very carefully. "Bangs" is a short, harsh word. It matches the sound of a noisy school bell.

"Slowly" and "sleepily" begin with the same letter. Poets often put sounds together like this.

Sounds Good
Poems are meant to be read aloud. You can almost hear the sound of the train when you read this poem by Robert Louis Stevenson, called "From a Railway Carriage."

PHOTOGRAPHY

Every day, more than 2 million photographs are taken around the world. These photos are not just snapshots of birthdays and holidays, but also pictures of goals being scored, models in studios, and important events. No matter how complicated the camera, all photos are made in much the same way as when the process was invented more than 150 years ago. A camera is basically a box with a hole in it. Light enters through this hole and shines onto the light-sensitive paper inside to form a picture.

Say Cheese!
In early photographs, it took a long time for the picture to form. People had to stay still for up to 20 minutes to keep the picture from blurring.

Flash

This tough camera will not break if it is dropped!

This spare camera has a long "telephoto" lens. It makes things that are a long way off look closer.

Lenses and lots of rolls of film are stored in this bag.

Click! A sinking bus is snapped.

Right Time, Right Place
Newspaper photographers have to be ready for action all the time. They may not get a second chance to snap an amazing event or famous person.

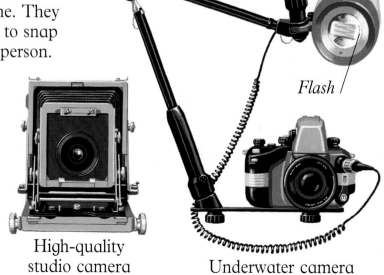

Flash

Camera Collection

35mm professional camera

Instant camera

High-quality studio camera

Underwater camera

This flash is much bigger than the flash on your camera!

Light bounces back off this board onto the person being photographed.

Lights, Camera, Keep Still!
Wind, rain, and poor light can ruin your shots when you take pictures outside. This is why photographers work in studios. Many of the pictures in this book were taken in a studio.

White paper reflects light back onto the model.

Small spotlights light up the white background.

The photographer takes pictures when the model is in the right position.

The person having a photo taken is called the model. You can see the final pictures of this dancer on pages 18-19.

Camera

An assistant hands film to the photographer.

This box is called a power pack. It provides the energy to run the flashes.

A cable connects the camera to the power pack. This makes sure the flash goes off when the camera clicks.

Spare film

The camera sits on a three-legged frame, called a tripod. This makes sure the camera does not move.

MOVIES

From the first flickery film, people have loved the world of movie make-believe. The early films were made in black and white and did not have any sound. They were called silent movies. In the theater, a pianist played along with the film, and the audience had to read words on the screen. It was not until 1927 that the first "talkie," called *The Jazz Singer*, came out. Color films, such as *The Wizard of Oz*, were made in 1939, but only became common in the 1950s.

A Star Is Born
The dry weather in California is ideal for filming. Hollywood, once a sleepy suburb of Los Angeles, was the center of the American film industry by 1920.

Silent Star
Charlie Chaplin (1889-1977) was one of the first movie stars. He starred in more than 80 movies. His most famous character was a little tramp who had a funny walk.

Cue Clapper Board
When a clapper board is clicked shut, it is seen on the film and heard on the soundtrack. The pictures and words can then be matched.

Moving Pictures
A movie is made of many still pictures, called frames. The frames pass before your eyes so quickly that the pictures look as if they are moving.

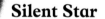

Small holes keep the film steady in the camera.

Frame

Eastern Promise
More than 800 movies a year are made in India – double the number made in Hollywood. Streets in Bombay and Delhi are lined with bright posters that advertise these dramatic movies.

The lighting crew sets up the lights so that the actor looks as if he is outside and not inside a bright studio.

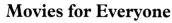

This "mountain" was built inside a studio.

The camera rolls forward on a wheeled truck, called a dolly.

Rain machine

Romance

Western

Horror

Science fiction

Between shots, the makeup artists make sure that the actor looks right.

This pole, which has a microphone on the end of it, is called a boom. It is held up high so that it does not appear in the movie.

The director is in charge of shooting the movie.

ANIMATION

Models and drawings can be animated, or brought to life on film. Drawings that move are called cartoons. This magic happens by taking photographs and making them into a movie. The models or drawings must be in a slightly different position in each picture. There are 24 pictures in each second of movement you see on screen and more than 65,000 pictures in a feature film!

© Societé de Produits Nestlé F.A.

Quick on the Draw

Many artists now use computers to draw cartoons. These Smartie candies were made to whiz through the air.

The clay face can be molded into a frown or a smile.

Move It!

This colorful model had to be moved and photographed more than 100 times to make it look as though it is turning around and walking toward the camera.

The model bends in the same places as a person. This makes it look more real when it moves.

Mortimer Mouse?

Mickey Mouse made his first appearance in the film *Plane Crazy* in 1928. His creator, Walt Disney, nearly called him Mortimer, but Mrs Disney suggested calling him Mickey Mouse instead.

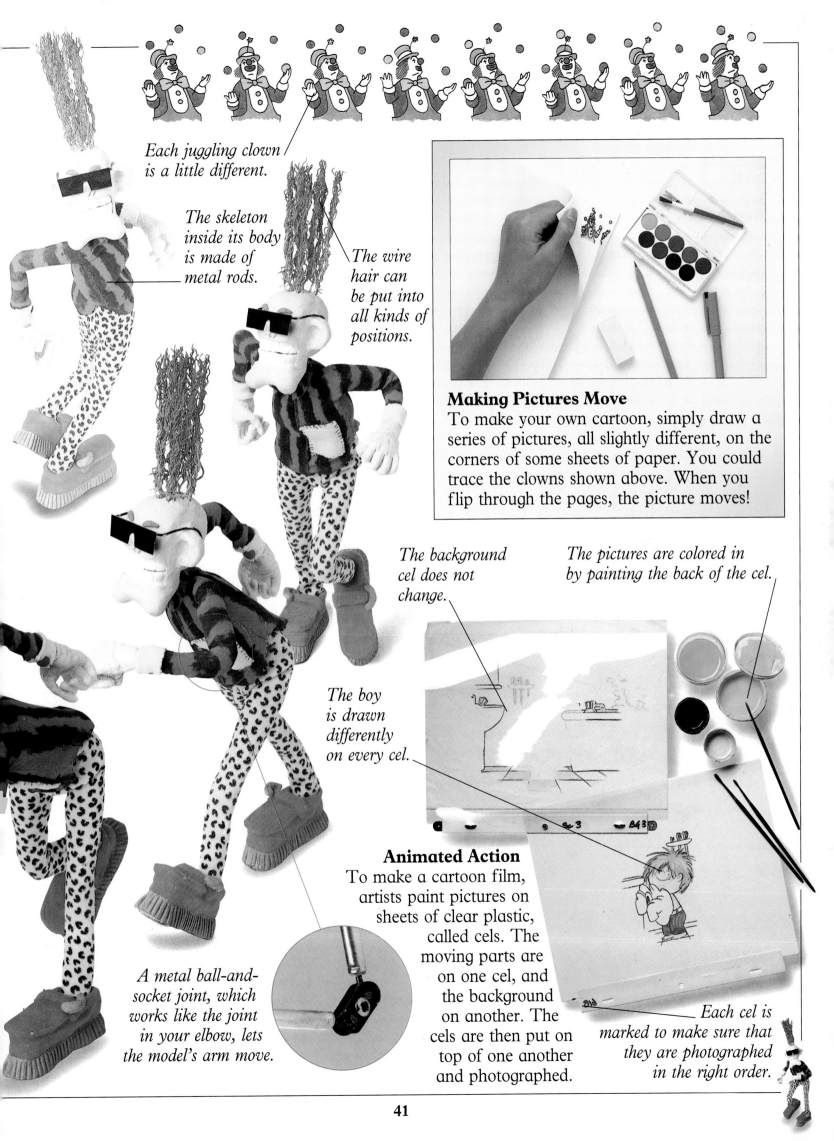

Each juggling clown is a little different.

The skeleton inside its body is made of metal rods.

The wire hair can be put into all kinds of positions.

Making Pictures Move

To make your own cartoon, simply draw a series of pictures, all slightly different, on the corners of some sheets of paper. You could trace the clowns shown above. When you flip through the pages, the picture moves!

The background cel does not change.

The pictures are colored in by painting the back of the cel.

The boy is drawn differently on every cel.

Animated Action

To make a cartoon film, artists paint pictures on sheets of clear plastic, called cels. The moving parts are on one cel, and the background on another. The cels are then put on top of one another and photographed.

A metal ball-and-socket joint, which works like the joint in your elbow, lets the model's arm move.

Each cel is marked to make sure that they are photographed in the right order.

SPECIAL EFFECTS

Have you ever wondered how alien worlds are filmed or how actors and actresses survive death-defying leaps? These amazing events are not real. They are created by special effects. With clever camera work and special equipment, such as wind machines, film directors can make us believe that what we are seeing is real. These tricks of the trade are used when shooting the action in the normal way would be too expensive, too dangerous, or just impossible!

Size Isn't Everything
This tiny, detailed model of a Y-wing spaceship appeared in *Return of the Jedi*. On-screen, it looked big enough to carry people!

A wind machine can make a gentle breeze or a howling gale.

Cue Weather
Filmmakers can't wait for the right weather. In this scene from *The Mosquito Coast*, giant fans whipped up the waves that battered the boat.

The lights shining through the glass look like real camp fires.

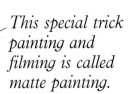

Blood Gun

The special-effects expert pulls the trigger to fire the red pellet.

People often have to pretend to be shot in films. Real guns can't be used because this would be too dangerous, so special blood guns are used. A small pellet is filled with red liquid. When this hits bare skin, it bursts and looks like a nasty bullet wound.

Air is forced down this hose to push out the blood bullet.

The highly trained stuntman leaps from the building.

The audience must think that the actor is falling, so the stuntman wears the same clothes.

Land of Make-Believe

This treetop village appeared in the movie *Return of the Jedi*. It was not built in trees, but painted onto glass! Small parts of the painting are scraped away, and live action is shown through these holes. In the finished film, actors, dressed as alien Ewoks, look as if they are in the village!

The stuntman waves his legs and arms around, to look as though he is terrified.

This special trick painting and filming is called matte painting.

The camera stops running when the stuntman prepares to land.

Fire!

Filmmakers don't just throw bombs to make flames and smoke. Explosions are carefully set up and controlled.

Fuse

Falling for You

Jumping from a high building is dangerous and difficult! In movies, it is only done by experts, called stunt people. They take the place of the actor or actress who is supposed to be falling to the ground in the story.

The stuntman twists in the air so that his shoulders will hit the bag first.

Smoke cylinders

Explosives

This can makes orange smoke.

Actor

The stuntman hits the soft air bag at more than 50 miles (80 km) per hour!

TELEVISION

In 1926, John Logie Baird screened the first pictures on his invention, the television. It was the birth of a whole new form of entertainment. The British Broadcasting Corporation started showing programs just ten years later. The magic of television is that you can see what is happening on the other side of the world without ever leaving your home. Often you see more of the event on television than if you were actually at the concert or beside the racetrack!

Today, almost all programs are made in color. CBS, an American television station, broadcast the first color programme in 1951.

The timekeeper makes sure that the program is exactly the right length.

2

Camera 2 focuses on the race cars as they skid around the first corner.

Sound engineer

The vision mixer switches the television pictures from one camera to another.

The director is in charge.

In Control

A team in the control room makes sure that the viewer gets the best possible pictures of events as they happen. On outside broadcasts, the control room can be inside a big van.

44

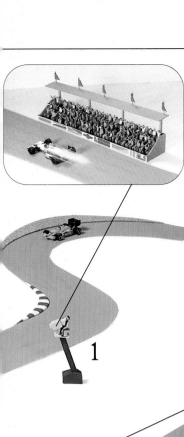

Camera 1 is on the start and finish line. It can show the reactions of the crowd as the cars flash by.

Camera 5 covers the action at the far end of the racetrack.

1

5

4

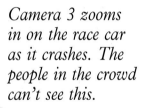

3

Camera 4 can see the cars as they come into the pits for new tires.

All-seeing Eyes

Cameras are carefully spaced all around the racetrack. They will be able to focus on everything that is happening on the track. Each camera sends its pictures back to the control room.

Camera 3 zooms in on the race car as it crashes. The people in the crowd can't see this.

1940s

1960s

1990s

Seeing Is Believing

Few people have the chance to swim through shoals of beautiful fish, but television can take you there.

Play It Again

Things can happen in split seconds. If you are watching TV, you can see a replay in slow motion.

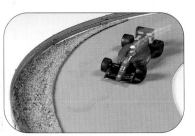

FUN AND GAMES

People have been playing games for thousands of years. From paintings and fragments found in tombs, we know that the Egyptians played board games 4,000 years ago. The ancient Romans, too, would meet at the baths to play dice. Chess was first played in India, in the sixth century. Today, the old games are as popular as ever, but new exciting ones, such as video games, are being invented all the time.

The chessboard is made up of 32 dark squares and 32 light squares.

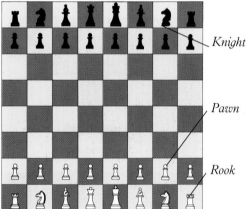

Knight

Pawn

Rook

Battle Plan

In the game of chess, two sides battle to capture one another's pieces. The first player to trap the other's king, a move called checkmate, is the winner.

The king can move in any direction, but only one square at a time.

The bishop is blocking the king's escape.

Wherever this black king moves, it can be taken. The white pieces have won.

This pawn has not moved during the whole game!

Time to Go

In 1857, a championship chess match took 15 hours. It ended in a draw. Players are not allowed to take this long today.

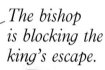

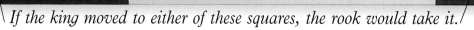

If the king moved to either of these squares, the rook would take it.

Roller Ball

In ancient Egypt, boys and girls used pebbles or nuts for playing marbles. Today we have glass marbles, which roll much more smoothly.

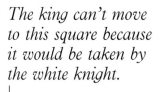

Modern marble

The Four Card Suits

Heart

Diamond

Club

Spade

Packed with Fun!

Hundreds of different games can be played with a pack of 52 playing cards. The European pack came from France around 1400, and the characters on the royal cards are still shown wearing the costumes from that period.

The next domino must have a blank side.

A "one" is always placed next to another.

The game starts with a high double, usually a six.

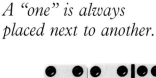

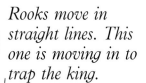

Join the Dots

Paper, and therefore packs of cards, used to be expensive. So poor people played dominoes instead. The dominoes could be made by anyone from wood or bone.

Knights move in an "L" shape.

Rooks move in straight lines. This one is moving in to trap the king.

The king can't move to this square because it would be taken by the white knight.

Screen Addicts

New technology has led to new games and new ways to play old games. In computer chess, you play against the machine, but can choose how hard the game will be! Unless they play very fast games, experts usually beat chess computers.

GLOSSARY

Amplifier A machine that strengthens the signals made by an electric instrument, such as a guitar.

Animation Photographing drawings and models to make them appear to move.

Bar A long, fixed pole that dancers use to help them do their exercises.

British Broadcasting Corporation (BBC) The British national television and radio company.

Brass instrument A musical instrument, such as a trumpet or a tuba, that is made of metal and played by being blown.

Canvas Material on which a painting is created.

Cel Clear plastic on which a cartoon picture is painted before it is photographed.

Checkmate The winning position in a game of chess, when a king cannot move without being taken.

Classical music Music composed in the late 18th and early 19th centuries, by composers such as Mozart. It is called classical music because it was inspired by ancient Greece and Rome.

Columbia Broadcasting System (CBS) A national television and radio company in the United States of America.

Comedy A performance that is funny or has a happy ending.

Composer A person who writes music.

Fiction Stories that are not true, but imaginary.

Flash A bulb that makes a sudden, very bright flash of light so that photographs can be taken when there is not enough natural light.

Frame A section of film. There are 24 of these pictures in every second of film that you see on screen.

Limelight A light that was used in theaters in the 19th century. Players stood in the limelight because it was the brightest part of the stage.

Metronome A machine that can be set to tick regularly at different speeds. Musicians listen to its beat to play at the right speed.

Mime A way of acting that uses movements and not words.

Nonfiction Writing that gives information and facts.

Overture The music at the start of an opera that introduces the tunes that are to follow.

Percussion instrument A musical instrument, such as a drum, triangle or cymbal, that is hit to produce sounds.

Portrait A picture or painting of a person.

Props Any small objects, such as books or pens, that are used in a photographic studio, play, or movie to make the scene look realistic.

Self-portrait An artist's picture of him- or herself.

String instrument A musical instrument with strings that can be plucked, like a guitar, or vibrated with a bow, like a violin.

String quartet A group of four string instruments playing together – usually made up of two violins, a viola, and a cello.

Symphony A long piece of music that is written for a large Western orchestra to play.

Telephoto lens The special part of a camera that makes distant objects look closer.

Tragedy A story that is very sad, or includes killing or death, and has an unhappy ending.

Woodwind instrument A musical instrument, such as a flute or a clarinet, that is played by being blown. Woodwind instruments used to be made of wood, but today many are made of metal.

Acknowledgments

Photography: Steve Bartholomew, Andy Crawford, Steve Gorton, and Tim Ridley.

Illustrations: Dave Fathers and Clive Spong.

Models: Donks Models.

Thanks to: Francesca Baines; Caroline Brooke; Sanjeevini Dutta; The Little Angels Puppet Theatre, London; Sandra Looke, Scallywags Child Model Agency; Samantha Webb; West Street Ballet School, London.

Text credits

"The Kite" from *Jungle Sale* by June Crebbin, © June Crebbin, 1988. Published by Viking Children's Books.

"Bells" from *The Wandering Moon and Other Poems* by James Reeves, © James Reeves (Puffin Books). Reprinted by permission of the James Reeves Estate.

INDEX

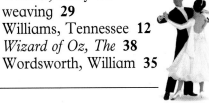